GOD'S DIRECT SPIRITUAL TEACHINGS AND TESTIMONIES

REV. DANIEL SANCHEZ, SR.

Inks and Bindings
888-290-5218
www.inksandbindings.com
orders@inksandbindings.com

CONTENTS

"God Doesn't Stop When Other Stop."

The Holy Spirit **Johns 16:13-15: of the truth, has come, He will guide you into all truth.**

A new life in Christi Jesus, with His Holy Spirit in our lives. If you are a person seeking to obtain understanding what God wants for you. Your best is to make a healthy relationship with the Holy Spirit.

According to God's grace given to you Holy Spirit will help you fill in all those blank spaces of questions you might have when you separate yourself and pray. Always pray with an open mind because that's when God will reveal to you. The word says that **we have not**, because **we pray not**.

It is a matter of believing, asking and being full of faith. Do not ever allow your faith to faint. As you become familiar with the Holy Spirit and its voice within your spirit becomes much easier to address with supplications.

It is not how some make it to be, to be led by the Holy Spirit, you need to realize that the Holy Spirit main objective is to lead you into the truth of God's will. By you being open minded and willing to be taught, the Holy Spirit will help you understand the proper foundation for God's ways.

A building with its different requirements to make strong, straight, character and purpose. That is what you need to understand about being tutored and trained by the Holy Spirit.

The Holy Spirit will not bend the rules nor stray away from who God is. He will challenge you to re-think some things.

1

"The Amazing Presence of God"

Makes you feel special, those moments when God improves you and reveals His authority in your favor. I have been challenged by many distinct types of witches, warlocks, voodoo and other types of false religions. Not something with which I had ever dealt with if you think about it why would we want to.

At my early stages of ministry, I notice that God had started to prepare me for such things. I did not know why? But God had started to introduce me to higher power fighting. It' a spiritual battle you encounter when dealing with demon spirits and other black magic type of witchcraft.

That reminds me of a night deep in sleep, I found myself in this dark place, but it was not here on earth. Reason I say that is because I found myself standing next to two male figures. One of them had a bullet hole on his shoulder.

While the other man placed his finger into the hole and twisted it to inflict pain. I looked over and stared at him, why are you doing that, and I continued with the question, where are we anyway? They both looked at me and both answered at the same time, nobody leaves this place once they are here. I asked why, and instantly looked around to see where I was.

All I could see was darkness and nothing made any sense. I answered back, saying I am not staying here, they both looked at me with a conniving grin. Once again, I looked to the left and to the right, all I could see was some type of houses but there was so much darkness, and it felt wicked, awful, ugly, and lost without saying a word I took off running.

By then it got darker, I could not even see my hand in front of me. As I ran, found myself running up hill. Then I came tumbling down, as I rolled and pulled myself up without the ability to see anything. I continued to run and again found myself going uphill. But this time I could sense and hear something chasing me, that thing was huge in weight and snored like a bull. But that time I knew it was the enemy **(devil)** chasing me.

By then I continued to run, feeling the heavy steps not far behind. I ran, I called to God for help and asked what is this thing after me, I kept going trying to get away from that place that those men had said nobody leaves.

Still completely dark and still rolling down those hills, every time I made it to the top of each hill, I could feel air space between my footing and my determination to keep my feet. I asked the Lord as I ran, what's the meaning of all this?

The Lord answered, in the ministry the church your called, you always feel the enemy trying to catch up with you. You will always be aware of his presence chasing you but know that he will not catch up with you.

We opened the church in June of 1986, Just as God said I have always felt the enemy's presence chasing always trying to cause problems, always trying to make things difficult, but God has always been right there leading the way. Always teaching revealing and exposing the enemy's plans. I had to learn to be sensitive and aware of the Holy Spirit revealing, guiding, and tutoring in things I did not understand after running all night, when I woke up the next morning.

Felt exhausted, bruised arms and legs from whatever it was, I had just experienced. I was young in faith, around four years into my Christianity when the Lord Jesus Christ was leading my wife and I into spiritual understanding, this experience I went through that night, has really explained and shared so much light into our walk in Christ.

These were experiences we just could not share with others at the time. First, they would not have believed it and second it was not something people would care to hear or understand at the time. But God knew that this type of Ministry would be needed for His people. Also, it is not a gift that you can grow into overnight. There is just so many things that need to be understood, the anointing plays an especially significant role, Spiritual growth is necessary. Your relationship with our Lord and Savior needs to be healthy because you will be challenged and tested by the adversary, throughout the years in our church ministry, we have felt the weight and pressure that comes from leading a church congregation.

"Holy Ghost Power"

I have heard over the years how this world and even Christians speak on the matter of the **Holy Ghost.**

As Christians ask for the **Baptism** of the **Holy Ghost** and evidence of speaking in **Tongues.** I thought as others that once you spoke in tongues, it was something you would do as needed, but the **Lord** and **Holy Spirit** revealed so much more unto my wife and I. The Lord taught me, that seeking the Lord in my prayer language **(Holy Ghost)** by listening to the Holy Spirit and the revelation of its awesome power. The channels of its communication, highlights and points of understanding.

It's streams of **Heavenly** waters continue to increase. This new and exciting manifestation took a very important role in our prayer and communication with our Lord Jesus Christ.

Holy Ghost Power, when your feeling defeated, weighed down; He will produce and strengthen you with fresh strength. When you pay close attention to His direction on things, situations and follow-up on His teachings. You will grow in knowledge of your **Christian Faith.**

One word given by the **Spirit** of our Lord and Savior Jesus Christ, opens new ways and doors to answers you been asking for. Don't rush into this but allow the **Holy Spirit** to set the pace. Learn to put **Jesus Christ** our **Lord** first in your life. You will start to see the difference in your daily living.

The Lord, Himself teaches unto us to separate and pray about things we're facing. Because **Faith** without works is dead. Challenge yourself to obey and follow the teaching of God. Allow your soul to rejoice and be filled with the **Goodness** of **God.**

Glory Full Gospel Church is a **Full Gospel Ministry Church.**

When God spoke the word **Full Gospel** unto my wife and I, I had never heard of such a ministry. I had gone before the Lord through prayer, asking what domination we were now, since receiving the **Baptism** of the **Holy Ghost,** His answer came instantly, you're now a **Full Gospel Church,** and you're going to operate in all five functions (anointing). When your young in the Lord, everything seems easy enough, but challenges come to learn that each anointing for each function was completely different, through all by the same spirit.

All this requires of your physical body differently, I'm just blessed God has always been so patient and loving through the whole process. I know some think there's no difference in operation, but **God** is a **God** of certain statures.

> **I Corinthians 2:12 Now we have received, not the spirit of the world, but the spirit who is from God that we might know the things that have been freely given to us by God.**

> **I Corinthians 12:28 And God had appointed these in the church: First Apostles, Second Prophets, Third Teacher, after that Miracles and Gifts…**

All these five-fold appointed positions take a certain heart with the Holy Spirit in the center of its operation. When you have walked, led by the Holy Spirit long enough, your being opened to the things of God that will take your breath away.

These things are what opens an incredible desire of faith to become that person God knows is real and truthful to God's calling.

We think we know what God wants of us in such callings, but you need to know you really don't have a clue what God has called you into. You're going to spend whole nights wrestling with your own self wanting to know how you're doing in this calling. You see callings works only when you put God first in your life. When you peel layers off yourself to make room for the thoughts of God.

From all the teaching, preachings and prayer you have encountered! It's God that opens those deep places in you to bring a new light in **Heavenly Places.** When that comes then you will understand the big picture of what God is doing in you.

All this that when you speak each word will have more of Heaven in it. A vessel of God enlightens the people of God. There's too much of man, men's ways and their ideas filling the churches of today. What's strange is that they don't even know it, they fought the Lord Jesus Christ when He walked and lived here on earth.

They question His teachings and ways, of the Lord's sayings and yet in the mid's of all this, the Lord continues to build His church. With patients you can run an excellent race, it's patients in all that you'll go through that will keep you in God's perfect will, because when your patience you learn to wait on the God, you'll learn the process of faith in a way that teaches you **wisdom.**

The five-fold ministry works your own heart first, it's like the veins in your body that supply blood throughout your body, the anointing of God will supply strength to you physically and spiritually.

When your body lacks strength, the anointing will activate strength into you. You're going to run into many **crossroads,** but God will lead the righteous.

> **I Corinthians 2:7-8 But we speak the wisdom of God in a ministry, the hidden wisdom which God ordained before the ages for our Glory. Which none of the rulers of this age knew; for had they known they would not have crucified the Lord of glory.**

> **Mathew 7:15-16 Beware of false prophets, who come to you in sheep's clothing, but inwardly they are ravenous wolves. You will know them by their fruits.**

In our walk with God being disciple by the Lord Jesus Christ, we have the witness throughout the time pastoring a church false prophets and wolves in sheep's clothing. Why is this so important today, because there's an increase of them. Something our Lord Jesus Christ revealed would happen is happening.

Those that are supposed to spot them don't. Christians need to know that thieves won't come and say, **I'm a thief.** Wolves in churches are operating and deceiving those that have been in Christ and church. The main problem is their discernment in the spirit is not being used or lack to know how, the main reason is, churches are not teaching how other churches don't operate or believe this is possible.

The operation of the Holy Ghost and the anointing of the Lord in churches is needed, the operation of the gifts as the spirit is God given for a special reason. They are not trophies to display, they are God given abilities to watch over the church.

We Pastor a church that meets every Tuesday on prayer and how to operate in discernment, how to use the Holy Ghost and power to receive answers on what to pray for. I have been taught through the Holy Ghost prayer how to be more effective on what to address in our prayers. How to find direction from our prayers, you can pray in the Holy Ghost and receive word of direction. That will open doors in heaven, open doors in front of you, open doors in your heart. This is more effective and better than just guessing on what to pray for. We shouldn't put limits on what God can do, the word says to some the thing of spiritual understanding is foolish because lack of faith and things of the spirit are spiritually discerned.

> **I Corinthians 2:14 But the natural man does not receive the things of spirit of God, for they are foolishness to Him nor can He know them, because they are spiritually discerned.**

This is really a more advanced way of praying. I give **Honor and Glory** to our Lord, through the Holy Spirit that taught us this method of prayer.

> **2 Corinthians 10:4-5 For the weapons of warfare is not carnal but mighty in God for pulling down strongholds. Casting down arguments, and every high thing that exalts itself against the knowledge of God, bring every thought into captivity to the obedience of Christ.**

"Holy Spirit Revelation"

Going back years when a close brother in Christ had not been seen my wife, Pastor Yolanda Sanchez mention that the spirit of the Lord had been placing brother (**we'll call him Sam**) in her spirit with concern. A week later I was seating in our living room, the time was around 2:00 – 3:00 pm when my wife comes out of the bedroom with great concern. She said the Lord through his spirit just revealed where Sam is, right this moment.

Bro Sam was in his early twenties and was a very gifted singer. His one of those that loved when people would receive him, and the God given gift of singing.

He had a gift of going into a church service and stir-up the spirit through **the God** given anointing. He would carry a briefcase of over two hundred cassettes. He could learn to hear a new song and memorize it completely. He loved singing for the Lord. On a Sunday Service he had shared with us, that he was helping and attending a church in the Houston area. We asked a few questions just to make sure he was being treated fairly. He couldn't stop expressing his excitement. But that's the last we heard of him. My wife said we need to hurry. What the Holy Spirit had revealed, she recognized the location and even the small church building. I stood up and said, I'm not even dress because I was wearing shorts, short sleeve shirt and house shoes. My wife Yolanda said, well just pass by the building and see if we can see him.

So, we got in the car and my wife drove toward the direction she had seen in the vision of God. It's amazing how the **Holy Spirit** can reveal when you connect with His ways and be sensitive to His voice. Like a doorbell at your home, someone rings it, and you open the door. Being familiar with how the Holy Spirit will reveal to you. I would never walk out of the house in shorts, but I could see my wife's concern. Finally, we got to the area and slowed down my wife said, I've seen the small building the spirit showed me.

Somewhere by the corner of this main street. There was a street that passed right next to the building. Now she drove very slowly, and we could see a door that was wide open on the side of that building. As we got right in front of that door, there he was singing on the altar. Somehow, he turns toward the door and saw us as we sat in our car. Somehow, he came to the door waved his hand, signal us to wait.

We didn't know how this would play out; I was blessed to see how God was helping. It was only God that Sam was able to see us by the curve parked. Five minutes later he comes running with his briefcase, climbing into the back seat. He said drive off; they are holding me hostage against my will. He said, I haven't eaten, and they keep me singing. We drove off to our home, and he shared everything he had gone through.

My wife asked him, where have you been staying? In Sinton, a neighborhood outside the city limits. Later that evening I drove him over to that house to pick up his clothes. He ran inside and came back quickly with his belongings. A man came to the door and look to see who drove him over there. But God is not limited, praise God my wife had already been praying for Sam and that everything turned out good. Our Brother Sam a few years later left to be with the Lord.

We do miss him, but the race continues. Brother Sam left a long-lasting expression of joy and memories in our hearts.

"CROSSROADS AND BRIDGES"

Some years later all this happened; we had another brother **(we'll call him Henry).** Brother Henry, when his parents both passed, he took it very hard. One day, he picked up and took off driving, his sister came to us and shared her concerns. How they hadn't heard anything from brother Henry and his where abouts and how they were worried about him. She asked if we could pray and ask God for answers, direction or insight. How this happened only God knows.

But I did pray, and God did answer. I looked at her and said his off on a main road near McAllen, Tx area. You'll find him there. They took off towards the area God had revealed through His spirit. We got a call that evening, and yes, they had found him. He was exactly where God had said.

Things like this continue to happen. We didn't know exactly how, but God was training us for bigger and greater things.

We became familiar with greater discernment and how the **Holy Ghost** was increasing in our walk with God. There's a lot of doubt and unbelieve in this world we live in.

But God is **Spirit** and the only way to discern spiritual is by the **Spirit of God**.

"DELIVERANCE AND RESTORATION"

O ne weekly workday we got a visitor come by the church office, the church secretary was finishing up her day, when someone knocked at the front church door. Secretary was by herself, not expecting anyone looked thru the small glass opening, there stood a young lady waving.

> **Johns 14:15-16 Points out that the Greek word for Holy Spirit can be translated into English in several different ways "Advocate", "Helper", "Counselor" and "Comforter".**

As to say please let me in. The secretary called me with a panic voice: Said Pastor there's a young lady in my office. I asked who she was but the secretary not knowing how to explain said, she's needing prayer. I asked what was going on? Secretary said, she's sitting up and wanting you to pray for her.

Little do we know, but God had led **(will call her Sis Martha)** into our church. Sis Martha mention that a close friend of Her's had informed her that **Glory Full Gospel Church** would help her deliver her of what was fighting against her. I told the secretary, tell her to come Tuesday for prayer meeting. I was out in the field working and couldn't pull away at the moment, not knowing what exactly was going on.

Sunday morning Martha and her husband came to church. She was still in panic mode, but very respectable. My wife and I pulled them into one of our classrooms to pray for her. That was the day **Sister Martha** and Her husband came into our lives.

The Lord cleaned her up in stages breaking down strongholds and the enemy had been attacking her continually (curses). That's when **Spiritual Healing** began in her and her husband. Her husband was always very quiet. Some members were very afraid of her at first; but her heart was in the right place. As weeks passed, they had become very faithful and committed to the church.

Sis Martha started to open up on past experiences, dealing with witchcraft. They and others spiritual problems attacked her daily. Both were there every service and Sunday School classes. My wife got very close to Sis Martha, she really was a very good person, they both were. Sis Martha mentioned how long she had been looking for help and deliverance. She had visited many churches, but none would or could help her. She was very loud, but full of encouragement and love for the Lord.

When she would step into the church, she was already praising God. Years later they found cancer fighting against her body. Sis Martha started her treatments and went thru a lot of pain, because the cancer was very aggressive spreading quickly. At the Dr's office the nurses that were treating her and giving her chemo treatments were stun, thinking she wouldn't make it another week for the following treatment: they were shocked (nurses) as she would walk in **Praising God.**

With all the pain, she looked stronger than the nurses themselves. Her body had weakened, she came on Tuesday for prayer meeting, and had lost a lot of weight. The week of Thanksgiving, we didn't know that would be the last time we would get to see her. Even when she was weak and tired Martha was encouraging others, witnessing about Christ. That night as they went home, she slipped and fell, her body was too weak to pull through she must have hit herself in the head.

God had brought this couple into our lives, were able to help them, truly she gave so much more in return. Sis Martha had become a very special friend to my wife, and our family. Even today we miss her dearly, for in such a short time she blessed our lives with her kind ways. Bro Joe **(her husband)**, since the day Sister Martha went to be with the Lord, has never stop coming, always the first one here and the last one to leave from every service.

The banner Sister Martha carried was passed over to her husband **(her testimony of giving).** He now helps serve in the church, he teaches, greets and helps in the Usher ministry.

I just couldn't write this book without honoring **Sis Martha** and how she lived for our **Lord Jesus Christ.**

"THE DAY GOD POPPED MY WHEEL ON MY LAWNMOWER"

John 15:12-17 The Lord God, speaks on us abiding in Christ and Christ abiding in us way to stay connected.

Brother Joe & Sister Martha were helping in raising and entrusted with the companion (**call him Fred**) of Brother Fred. He was at least 55 years old and been entrusted into Sister Martha's care. Fred had lived with Bro Joe and Sis Martha for over 10 years Brother Fred was older than Brother Joe and Sister Martha, but that didn't face them; He was blessed to have a family. He called them Dad and Mom, since the day we met them. Well, my point is this; Fred had started working with me at a Construction sites, he was very good at cleaning and helping (**I gave credit to Brother Joe and Sister Martha for teaching him**).

One Saturday morning I called and asked Brother Fred if he wanted to come help me cut my yard, he always wanted to work and gladly accepted. I went over and picked him up that Saturday morning. I pulled the lawnmower out and the weed eater. I was standing about five feet from Brother Fred, I mention to him there's the lawnmower go at it, Brother Fred said **NO!** I'm a pro with the weed eater that's how I cut my grass at home besides that's how I have been trained at the air base on how to cut it all with the weed eater.

Brother Fred has a disability and was disabled to understand certain things. Not wanting my grass tortured, my lesson for pushing

16

was to teach him, but he refused I said no you're cutting with the lawnmower. This went on for some fifteen minutes, by then I was standing behind my lawnmower and pushed it towards him. I made a slight push and off went the lawnmower towards Brother Fred.

Brother Fred was looking at the lawnmower, suddenly, I got this strange feeling, like God was saying let him do as he knows and stop pushing him (Fred) to do it your way a few minutes later as I looked at Fred to see what he would do.

A beam of strong force was felt I saw a thin ray of lighting come from the sky and hit the front of the lawnmower I heard a sharp but loud sound as a rod of lighting hit the tire, the tire flew up about three feet off the ground. All this happening like in slow motion, then the tire came back down spinning, came to a rocky type motion and stopped like when you lay a plate down, but it does a walking type movement.

Brother Fred stepped back with his hands up in the air and said, I didn't do it. I looked at him and then turn my attention back to the wheel of my lawnmower. Fred was still saying he hadn't done it. I said Brother Fred its ok, just cut the grass as you have been taught. I pushed the lawnmower over to a side picked up the wheel that flown up in the air.

I looked at it, and said **OK God** I got the message, but God had been there watching us the whole time. The Lord had told me to stop insisting for Fred to use the lawnmower.

Bro Fred had to move when Sister Martha had gone to be with the Lord, they are indeed missed. But God does watch over his children and some. I haven't seen Bro Fred since, but I can tell the impact of losing Sister Martha, his known mom has taken some toll on him. My wife and granddaughter ran into him (and a supervisor) at a local store, but Brother Fred didn't recognize them.

But the compassion and love God has for His children is above anything were familiar with. God shows us His love every day, but this life we live tends to hinder and we sometimes lose sight of God's compassion and mercy.

> **Hebrew 1: 8-10 But to the Son He says: your throne, O God, is forever and ever. A scepter of your Kingdom, you have loved righteousness and hated lawless therefore God your God, has anointed you with the oil of gladness more than your Companions. You Lord in the beginning laid the foundation of the earth and the heavens are the works of your hands.**

At day one, when God called **Glory Full Gospel Church** into existence, my wife and I were very young, given a great responsibility. How God knows who and what is needed for us to weather the storms ahead. Pastoring a church is a calling that requires more than anyone can prepare for. But God knows how to make things a little better; God had my in-laws, and my parents join us since day one. Two couples that were completely different in their own ways, but they were the source (as some would) needed to encourage, support and help in this new venture. They never left until the day God called them home. There was so much work to do; we build, worked, constructed according to needs.

We dealt with church problems, different family problems, financial problems and they never did quit nor complained. They were prayer warrior's: the men would meet at early hours to pray for the church and the people, early hours were 4:30 – 7:00 am twice a week at times. Our moms would come into the church and pray, they would both take a certain side of the church and pray for every pew and person that would sit on those pews.

We all worked together for God, His church with great joy, sometimes we would sit in the church laugh, share, rejoice and at times wondered how and what else would challenge our **Faith.** They never missed services; we're talking over twenty to thirty some years.

We lost my mother first in the month of November 2020. Then both our fathers around five years ago, lost both about a month apart.

We did the services for Pastor Yolanda's dad; Brother Richard had been taken from us in November 2017. A month later my father, Pedro also went to be with our Lord in January 2018. A few years ago, my mother in-law Sister Janie was called by God to go home.

Sis Janie, I'm guessing 4' 10" inn height. But she was something else in prayer, she wouldn't hesitate when called to pray. At time I would go by her house and ask her to pray for me. She would shake you and rebuke the enemy she wasn't afraid of spiritual combat, actually she loved it. We extremely miss them now God had placed these four wonderful people, our Parents to help us on this great commission.

We know they're in a better place now, but we still miss their company, their laughter, their smiles, their special ways of understanding, forgiving and embracing this high calling of God. They all were so different and yet so bonded in the love of God.

"GOD CALLS, BUT IT'S UP TO US TO LISTEN."

My parents and my in-laws with a desire to serve, not even trying to do things for God to be recognized. But it was them that activated the ministry of prayer in our church. My father in-law activated the video ministry at the church, with a video track camcorder device, he set the tripod in place and started recording and the church aired in a religion city cable channel. This generation of God fearing, God giving servants will be missed. A distinct generation with their hope of faith to see the mighty miracles of God honor faith. They were still blessed and pleased to witness the Glory of God.

Now we move into this new generation with the task to teach and educate, but God has raised the bar and even increase the anointing. Requires an increase in our faith, increase in our obedience and increase our actions of faith.

God has honored our faith in many victories of battling against the power of darkness. It's said that churches chose not to believe in such captivity that Christians suffer from, church going sons and daughters of God are faced with. Being native to such forces is a sin itself; because how can we ignore the responsibility of watching over the flock of God. Recently my wife and I received a higher calling give and granted by God.

God see what we're faced with, different challenges with the increase of darkness, things are happing in this life (**world**)that had never been seen before. Different types of **Black Magic, Witchcraft,**

Voodoo and Sorcery that has been passed down from generation to generation.

Just recently we came across a certain type of called Christians. Within their worship and praise behind the scenes they practice a type of witchcraft we haven't seen before. If your familiar with operating in the spiritual, supernatural realm, the gift of discernment gives your eyes to see even what you cannot see in the natural. Discernment exposes the tactics of the devil or of those that practice witchcraft. In serving the church of God, we through God's anointing have set many captives free.

Through God we have delivered many who were in bondage of witchcraft and other strongholds set by darkness, curses, witchcraft and other operations. We have witness people poses with demonic spirits. Through the power of faith, God's anointing and prayer many have been set free.

Our Lord Jesus Christ through the process of time has taught us and equipped us with a stronger anointing to help overcome the challenge that comes, while serving God's purpose in these latter days.

I write this that you may understand that the challenges of a church body have increase and change, due to latter day of fulfillment of prophecy. Seem that winter days have come and new challenges that we have been running into. Recently we have had to deal with an Ancient Egyptian witchcraft spirit. When we ran into this challenge, we were not aware of its existence.

Glory Full Gospel Church is a family church with Sunday School departments in operation. Our main goal is to lead people into a new life **(Born again believer)** with our Savior Jesus Christ. Salvation and ministering the word of God is our main goal. But to minister the fullness of God's word, we operate in the five-fold ministry. The **Apostle** ministry (God's foundation for the church) the **Prophet** ministry (seer for the body of Christ), the **Evangelize** ministry (to edify and unite in faith), the **Teaching** ministry (advocate, give understanding), **Pastoral** ministry (shepherd the flock of God).

But the church of today is being targeted by wolves in sheep clothes, by witchcraft more open than ever before. All this has been around since the early church, but the enemy being aware of the signs of time is attacking the church of today. The things that happening around the world speaks for itself that our Savior is coming soon. Nobody knows for certain when, but the evidence of wars and rumors of war, flooding as never seen before are things the word of God speaks of, that His time of His coming is drawing near.

Now back to Ancient Egyptian Spirit, that was attacking our family and church. We could discern its presence it's movement and the Spirit of our Lord Jesus Christ was exposing its actions.

But we were having trouble locating it, plus the power of this spiritual darkness was causing many problems (stirring problems). We asked the Holy Spirit what was coming against us. Through the Holy Spirit and discernment, we could feel it's presence but couldn't find evidence of its location first. My wife has a very strong discernment of enlightenment of seeing in the spiritual. She works as my eyes, I must operate by faith, discernment and movement to identify the attacker.

It's the only way I can explain this matter. Well, this time she wasn't seeing anything of what was attacking us. God taught us to operate as one, but this was a first to be challenged on this type of tactics. What we did was ask the Holy Spirit to expose the source we were up against. The Holy Spirit identified the type of darkness we were up against. He said Ancient Egyptian Spirit was what this group was operating in. Once we located the intruder and its power, now we knew what we were up against.

This made it possible to tract down; in the spirit we located the area of location it was a cave on the outer part of a certain town. What was happening, we would witness the Rock type door slide up and down. They would go in and out, invisible you could say. It was the Holy Spirit that helped us bind them, it took some getting used to, but as soon as we had them binded, we could locate and see their presence.

Ugly looking, representing different creatures walking on two legs, this battle went on for a few weeks. We were able to track them down to where the core of the operation was located in. Our Lord Jesus Christ has taught us that prayer has many doors. There's prayer to address and ask God for different types of help.

But that there's prayer for Spiritual guidance, that helps and teaches on how to handle spiritual problems and the power of darkness.

Just the idea to ignore its existence; witchcraft powers of darkness, etc. doesn't mean it doesn't exist. Even our Lord Jesus Christ was confronted, and He rebuked with authority demon activity. I know this type of Ministry is not for everybody. But that doesn't mean it's not needed, and that Christians will need help.

One thing to understand is that the enemy's main goal is to destroy and hurt the body of Christ. Which is the church. Remember the people of God are the true church. The enemy is coming after the body of Christ; that doesn't mean He'll win, but He wants to cause damage to you and your family. His main objective is to steal, kill and destroy. How does he do all this? By cursing, deceiving, breaking heart, and inflicting pain of infirmities and diseases.

But God has given us gifts and **Holy Ghost Power** through faith that moves mountains. We just need to obey, believe, pray and act on our faith towards God.

Ephesians 6:12 For we do not wrestle against flesh and blood, but against principalities against powers rulers of the darkness of this age against spiritual hosts of wickedness in the Heavenly places.

Recently, after years of hearing the term; Principalities in high places. Well recently we were dealing with some Ancient Egyptian witchcraft. This ancient witchcraft spirit that was coming against us. Spiritual battles sometime the only way to overcome or stop, takes inside from God and understanding into God's mysteries. One thing to understand is when we open the door to help and minister to those that are demon possessed, cursed with witchcraft, need deliverance and the breaking of strongholds, etc.

Whatever power of darkness we break, remove or stop. Retaliation does come at times. So that's how we had to battle against the ancient Egyptian spirit. My wife and I address the heavens of God for direction on this matter. The **Holy Spirit** directed us to the place. To our surprise, we came face to face in the spiritual with the location of principalities in high places. As we arrived at the location, we stood on a high place on a Hill over seeing this place. To give a comparison, it looked like looking at Houston, Texas. With huge buildings and very large, the air was thick and black.

My wife said the smell was terrible and hard to tolerate, I mention we better go and get this done. This is not a place to enter for the faint in heart. We go because our faith in God says He won't let us do something we can't handle. We entered some huge building, that let us into a huge area (coliseum type. We both instantly knew what this meant.

I spoke to my wife and said, something is coming on our right side. Its footsteps are huge and heavy. She looked and said yes, it's in the shape of a bull walking on two legs. Spiritual fighting is different than what some think. This spirit fights with power of darkness and abilities they have acquired through time.

This bull thing spoke and said in surprise, where did you come from? Haven't seen a human in this place for a very long time. In this deep strange voice, and no human has ever left this place. I said, I come in the Name of our Lord God. He took a few steps back and I charged at him, with weapons that God had train us over the years. That thing was about thirty-five feet tall.

That day it fell, on the way down he made a sound out, like a whistle type sound. That sound called another creature out from the opposite side of the arena, this time it was a huge dragon type creature with some ugly looking horns. My wife said, there's a huge dragon that just came out behind you. I turned and moved toward its direction and again I found myself fighting. We defeated that one as well. When we were done, and we started to make our way out.

God sent a strong wind and swept us quickly from that place, the only reason I share this is because people lack to believe and understand the true prize that the true servants of God pay. We must endure and overcome certain challenges.

(This principalities in high places) It's like the main offices of the power of darkness that operate over the earth. This place you won't find or see, unless God allows it.

Our God has honored our faith, mainly His words, in many victories of battles against the power of darkness. It's sad that certain denominations and churches chose not to believe in such captivity that Christians church going sons and daughters of God are attacked with. Many suffer from this and seek help. How can we ignore the responsibility of watching over the flock of God. Recently and often our Lord, our God increases His anointing, His Holy Ghost Power, His wisdom and gifts to equip us for the task at hand.

God see's what we're face with, different challenges with the increase of darkness here on earth.

We have pastored for thirty-seven years. Through those years Our Lord Jesus Christ, through His Holy Spirit has taught, train and revealed the effective revelation of the Holy Ghost. How to address the manifestation of the Holy Ghost. How to address our attention in the process of prayer and connection with its revelation knowledge.

How the Holy Ghost directs us to whatever He feels we need to know, and what needs to be address or overcome. The Holy Ghost reveals inside on circumstances and other much needed guidelines to solving problems.

I praise God for His patience in teaching us. Revealing wisdom and knowledge are God given. Think about it, we're ready to believe things on this earth that we haven't even seen. We're ready to make acceptations on what some claim to be; observation on what some believe and yet not proven. People come with some, don't make sense doctrines and people run with it.

I know that some Christians spent a lifetime educating themselves in the word of God, and there's nothing wrong with education but the word of God is like a map, a gate way into the fullness of God's truth. The Holy Spirit of God leads you into a greater measure of **Understanding**. The Holy Spirit leads into the God given **Grace.**

This **Grace** used correctly can lead into greater **Knowledge** of God's will for you and others. The grace of God can help your growth into a better **Relationship** with God for forgiveness of all wrong doings and ready to walk in His Righteousness.

"True Living Waters"

Theres is hope for us after all. The reason I say this is because people are blinded by whatever circumstances they have lived by. After time it starts to mole their thinking and faith. But if you're ready to have pure faith in God.

God will help you awake from all things that are troubling you. He will heal your land (meaning you), that's when revelation of God makes its way into your life as never before. I'm telling you of something I have tested, proven and lived. I'm sharing with you on how to find the power of revelation. The **Power** of God given truth.

It will teach you a different site of the Holy Ghost that you might have never known. All these are the true living waters from the presence of God. I'm not questioning your faith but trying to enlighten your walk with God.

"Living Waters"

Your thirst will be quenched: Is when your calm down in heart, soul and mind, and you'll find peace a of grace that refreshes your entire human and spiritual being. All this will open your faith, your heart and mind for more of God. When the Holy Spirit starts flowing in you as it is supposed too. Then you'll understand what I'm trying to enlighten you in. Why am I doing these? Because it's time, God wants His people (sons & daughters) to have a better understanding. What well better work for them. It's sad that many churches have taken teaching the things of God, for their own personal gain. But that's something they will have to answer to God for. My commission is to bring you into the understanding of God's spoken word and request.

The Lord Jesus Christ is releasing living water for His children to overcome what their faced with today. This water is to quench and stop what's stealing your blessings. To refresh your soul and enrich your faith, to awaken you from whatever it is your facing or going through.

Sometimes we miss what the problem is especially when we're blinded by man's doctrines. It gets in the way of all that God wants for you. We hear certain things but lack to understand because mentally were already going the opposite direction. We think we know, but truly don't have the whole answer.

If you stop all those horses that are pulling you in all directions. Give God some of your time. The answer of the Holy Spirit leading you into God's grace, will give you what you need to succeed and overcome. Take some time off from trying to make things happen. Open your heart to God, allow the Holy Spirit to show you how to stand in faith. In this stand you take, should align you're hearing into a better search of God's riches. This is going to test your patience and your want.

Your patience with this process, you'll start to see some changes for the better. Your confidence in this approach will grow because you'll find it rewarding how well God teaches, reveals; these steps will help to attain what's in your heart desires.

> **Jeremiah 33:2-3 "Thus says the Lord who made it the Lord who formed it to establish it (the Lord is His name). Call to Me, and I will answer you, and show you great and mighty things, which you do not know."**

The Power of Heaven is given to enlighten and to help. Life has so many obstacles, but God works through incentives. Because He believes in giving and helping to encourage. If we place close attention to the Holy Spirit in our Christian life. The **Holy Spirit** is about helping us to understand how to make better decisions. Also how to know what God gives us to overcome whatever is hindering us. More than anything else is to stop what the enemy uses to steal, kill and destroy whatever accomplishments we've had. The enemy destroys **Relationships** and whatever else he can accomplish against us. Is it asking for too much that God offers His help that we're not condemn for life.

God even offers a better future in heaven. If we chose to take what His willing to give us, a **Hope** that comes through His Resurrection Power. Our Lord Jesus Christ gives us His love if we chose to believe His good news. Seems like this world continues to prefer misery, rather than the Holiness of God's goodness. It's funny how people try to find fault on something that' so pure and innocent.

Our Lord Jesus Christ is our **Creator**, our **Salvation, Lord and Savior.**

Matthew 9:12-13

Jeus heard that, He said to Him "Those who are well have no need of a physician but those who are sick. But go and learn what this means; "I did not come to call the righteous, but sinners, to repent."

Our Lord Jesus Christ seeks those that are looking for help. That can see the truth in Himself, how God can strengthen, motivate and build one's heart desires. As the word says, if you think your perfect and there's no room for changes. When you feel you never do any wrong or hurt others by your way of talking. We don't look for help, when having such a mindset.

We lack to see, believe in what God can do for us. But when you want help even though you're not a terrible person. When we put all our attention to working, and never pick up our heads to the life that's passing us by.

Without realizing or considering we get blinded to what real living should be. Pressure and problems have a way of changing us to become something we always said we wouldn't. That's why being in church on a steady pace, works in your favor. The Holy Spirit of God the living word of God, Ministers to our soul, heart and mind.

The word reminds us of true values and bring **Peace** back into our hearts, ministers unto every part of our living, **Physically** and **Spiritually.** Through God being in our lives, the living waters of God, waters our lives. When we apply and make effort to hear what God through His Holy Spirit is saying. We the branches of God, begin to produce fruit of the ways of God.

The love of God begins to manifest more and more, as we get ahold of our Lord's sayings. When we can see for change and open our hearts to the Lord's word, there's no limit to what God can do for us. Your branches will be filled with the fruit of the **Holy Spirit.**

John 3:16

For God so loved the world that He gave His only begotten Son, that whoever believes in Him should not perish but have everlasting life.

I praise God for this great journey, that He chose. From the first day, till this very day. God continues to teach us and reveal unto us, His very will. One day as we seeked the Lord Jesus Christ for guidance and direction: the answer of the Lord came; know that in this house (the church). There's a ladder connected to the heavens. Angels with ascending and descending from the heavens. In those answers of God, we have witness and learn a close relationship with our God.

My wife and I have come to understand and see great wonders of God. With each revelation, witness and vision. We have come into a fast-growing pace. How God builds a **Church**, how He address the body of believers and how He makes known what He wants done. As to how the people of God refuse what God wants for them. In each mind, people assume what they think and want to believe.

All this didn't start just recently but has been going on since the beginning of God's creation. Mankind have managed to stay away from a path of God. However, it might sound and yet the earth has so many **Denominations** present to this day. Now that we have a better understanding of things to keep in mind and know that there's always a need to stay focus, cause things will come and move you always from your **Faith** in God. Always trying to infect you with worldly thinking. Anything that can keep you from truly obeying our Lord and Savior.

The cross that our Savior faced to defeat the power of death and sin. When our Lord Jesus Christ overcame death, it's been given to us the resurrection power of living a better life through Christ Jesus. These born-again experiences give a greater **Hope** for now here on earth and some day in heaven.

"SIGNS & WONDERS"

In our Christian walk, there's never a dull moment. There are always new challenges popping up. The church was going through a certain phase, no matter how much I tried to address the problem. Seem like nothing was working, I just couldn't understand why they didn't care to change their ways in seeing the problem. The problem was that the enemy had been putting fires between certain members.

We would put one out and another would manifest this went on for some time. It wasn't enough to destroy the church, but enough to cause problems between family members. There was time, they didn't' care to serve with each other. It seems like everyone had a perfect reason and they weren't backing off. We felt like what could we do to keep the peace and stop the tactics of the enemy.

We knew who was behind it, but it wasn't helping matters that people always are able to say the wrong thing at the wrong time. We prayed to God about this matter, and He said, I have defused it. Just as God said, this problem stopped. But what it had damaged or hurt I could still see the evidence. After enduring for so long, on day as I was about my daily work, I question my **Faith** in a way to see what God would do. Well without realizing what I had done and its effects.

I knew my faith was down, but I couldn't explain how. A few weeks later as I was praying, I would get this image in my Spirit of a river and clear water rushing by. In this clear water I could see a reflection deep in the bottom of this river. For weeks every time I prayed there was the same reflection. So, what I did as I prayed-put my head into the water.

It must have been about 8 feet deep, and I drew closer to that reflection. There it was a shiny shield half stuck in the bottom on a bed of rocks. Not knowing what this meant, I left it there. However every time I would pray, there it was again like as it was telling to get it. This went on for another week, as I was driving, I said unto the Lord I feel like of lost the **Power of Faith.** That's when He (Lord) said, I've been telling you and showing you where it is.

That's when I understood what that shiny reflection meant. I said to the Lord I'm sorry, and I remembered without thinking, when I dropped it. That afternoon I got home, I separated myself and prayed. There it was my **Sheild of Faith** deep in the crystal-clear water. I picked it up and instantly my Spirit was quicken and my **Faith** was back locked in place.

Who would have ever thought, how we can let go **Faith** not realize the power of our words. I had notice that I had been getting banged up frequently and knew something must be missing in me. We don't realize how much our **faith** in God **protects** us daily.

That was a big teaching for me and shed a lot of light on what we acknowledge or say without giving it a second thought. I'm **Grateful** to God and His **mercy** as to how He **protects** us and lets us see our **foolishness** on what we speak out. We seem to take things for granted and think nothing can hurt us. Praise God for His **mercy**, **grace** and the **Holy Spirit** that He reveals to us there more we need to learn and know.

Teachings like this, opens your mind and heart for greater things of God. Because we're always asking God for more **anointing**, more **authority** and mor **Holy Ghost.** But as we learn where we have failed and realign our ways of talking, seeing things make us more ready for greater things of God. That day, I hadn't lost faith in God, but in myself. That's why my defense was gone. That shield of faith was down in the bottom of the crystal-clear living waters of life.

I know better now and hopefully this will never happen again. There are things of the heavens that people don't know, nor speak off.

But what I will tell you, it's more beautiful, huge and full of **Glory** than one could ever imagine.

The doors to the court room, and different chambers, in the heavens are seventy feet tall. The **Angels** are about that size as well. There's's healing rooms that as you get into its waters, looks like pools for one person. There're some pools for several people. But when you come out of those living waters, your healed, restored and ready for more. The Lord has revealed this to us because of what we must endure and overcome.

After so many battles we need help and restoration. One day the Lord took us there, He said we had been facing a lot of adversity. We both felt broken, tired and without strength. Theres more to the Heavens, than what I chose to share. But I want you to know there is better place waiting for us in heaven one day.

The way there's different departments and offices, court houses and capitals here on earth. There are different chambers, court rooms and buildings. Just like Jesus Christ said, I the gospel of **John 14:1-6 I go to prepare a place for you, in my Father's house are many mansions.**

There are many mansions way greater, better and more beautiful than we can imagine.

John 3:9-12

Nicodemus answered and said to Him, "How can this be?"

Jesus answered and said to him, are you the teacher of Israel, and do not know these things? Most assuredly, I say to you. We speak what we know and testify what we have seen, and you do not receive our witness. If I have told you earthly things and you do not believe, how will you believe I tell you heavenly things?

When the Lord Jesus Christ told Nicodemus about being born again. Nicodemus couldn't' see how that was possible. That's how we sound when told of something we're not familiar with. But really its lack of faith or believe in our part. This Christian walk we're in is about faith in God. Believing the report of God made know unto us. The word says that God ministers unto us through preachers. Yes, that God sent preacher with the good tidings of good news.

THE SPIRIT OF WISDOM

God's mysteries continue to come, in the early hours around one o'clock in the morning. I was semi awake and half asleep when I found myself by a small pond of water. There I stood starring at this huge rock type structure. This huge stone had scratch marks on its face rugged surface, like a huge paw (like bear claw) had a swing at it. This rock structure was standing by this small pond.

The pond must have measure ten feet by ten feet, no more than, one hundred square feet in size. The water must have been about five feet deep. There I stood wondering the meaning of these that I was witnessing. I could see some small fish swimming in its waters. I looked around to see exactly where I was. All I could see was a sloppy flat land all around. Then from nowhere I saw a man coming towards me with a beard down to His mid-section. His hair and beard were a white radiant looking color. His hair was long to his waist as well.

He asked if He could get a drink of water from the pond. I shook my head up and down to indicate yes. He said I been walking for a long time. I asked Him where are you coming from, and who are you? He replied I go through and fro the earth to see who will receive Me. My name is **Wisdom**. I'm the spirit of wisdom. He also mentions, it's been a while since anyone received (Me) and gave me some water to drink.

Wisdom was at least six feet to six feet four inches tall. He was slim and spoke calmly, but with a lot of **Authority.** I still wasn't sure what all this meant or why. He spoke with me and knew who I was. I notice that He would answer me only after I would ask questions. As time went by, in my prayer time I would go to the same spot by faith.

I started to notice the rock wasn't as rough as before and that the pond was getting bigger in size. I asked Wisdom what this rock represented. I notice that the scratches were fading away. The spirit of Wisdom answered and said, this stone rock represents the church your pastoring in. Also, the water represents the living water of God in the church. As your growing and ministering the living water is increasing as well.

The scratch marks are fading away, because the church is getting healed from the **hits** and **damages** the enemy had attacked the church. Now there was a young tree growing by the pond, Wisdom said this young tree is the children of God that are growing in the church. The Lord God our savior Jesus Christ once again had sent us help. The spirit of wisdom as I would come through prayer to this certain location. He would help me by answering questions I had about things the church was faced with.

As I would arrive, I would look around for Him. Then I would see the spirit of Wisdom appear. He would always be willowing on a stick as He looked towards me, as to say how are you? Throughout the years that stone grew and the pond as well. That tree by the pond was growing and spreading its branches. I would look at the living water of the pond and the fish had now grown as well. I was **blessed** to have this time with the spirit of **Wisdom.**

He would help me in things that I needed answers for. What was so awesome was to hear Him, the answers that came from those encounters. Till this day I still go seeking the spirit of **Wisdom.**

In some of those answers going through time and understanding things, from a greater, higher perspective. What's so amazing is that God has never left Me nor forsaken us. The Holy Spirit of God has always made a way to help and minister to us. On a certain service as I was preaching on a Sunday morning when suddenly, I witness a ray of light enter the center of the church. In the midst of the congregation the spirit of **Wisdom** came and sat on one of the center pews.

I looked around to look at the people, The Sons and Daughters of God to see if they had notice Him **(Wisdom).** But nobody turns to His direction. That night as I sat at home, the spirit of Wisdom spoke to me. He said, did you notice that nobody saw Me. I said yes, I did notice that nobody turns to look at you.

Wisdom said that's how it is around the world; I can go and look into churches, and they don't notice Me. He also said but you saw Me come in. I said yes, I saw your **Glory** of light come and visit the church. All these things that God teaches and makes available are to **test** the body of Christ. I have also seen the spirit of our Lord Jesus Christ visit the church during service time.

It's one of those things that you'll never forget. He won't even say a word but looks around at the congregation. Or he'll stand on the altar as the group is playing, singing praise and worship.

We're so blessed to have such a wonderful, amazing God that loves us more than we know. To witness His concern for mankind is something in itself. When I been preaching and at times prophesying, I witness the Lord yearn for His people. His concern or desire for them to understand what's at stake.

When the spirit of our Lord moves in our heart through His spirit. It gives us a glimpse of His great love for mankind and His children.

Many of a time the Lord has shared with me; He'll say as you preached my word and spoke to their hearts; now we'll wait to see if they will listen. Many times, the Lord has said, I have shared with them by dreams and visions what I want them to do. But they refuse to listen or obey.

"HOWEVER"

However, is the word that better describes the times were living in. People want to believe on what they make themselves to believe. But the truth is that Jesus Christ came into this world to open understanding with His truth. There was nothing normal as to what Jesus Christ did when here on earth, walking in the flesh. He came into this earth born of a chosen young lady called Mary, a virgin. At the age of thirty-three years of age He revealed the main true reason His Father God sent Him to live among the people here on earth. He brought the living word with power and might.

Even those that tried to oppose Him fell short. How could they stop the acts of supernatural? The deaf could hear the mute talked, the blind could see, the cripple could walk and many more acts of wonders He did to reveal that God through His Son, Jesus Christ walked here on earth. You're always going to have the doubters. But for those that chose to believe, a new way, a certain message of Hope was God sent.

A Gospel of truth with salvation for mankind was present. The supernatural of God's power with evidence of Holiness was now here on earth. The word of God says that He gave gifts to His chosen children. Why people chose not to believe is beyond me. Because the Holy Spirit and the word of God came with power. Giving testimony of God and His kingdom.

That's why I named this chapter **However.** The Lord Jesus Christ through His mercy and grace has revealed, shown mighty things. He has taken us by the hand to enhance, enlighten and educate through His Holy Spirit. I'm so grateful for His patience in the process of teaching and making us see what so many fail to understand. The Lord has built our faith over and over again.

I still remember when we first began and now admire how the Lord manage to open our eyes to see mighty things of His Kingdom. How His taught us to see through His spirit, we can claim whatever we think, but its faith in God that moves mountains. The more you understand the stronger your faith will become.

Throughout the years His manage to open a greater understanding as we have walked in this chosen path of God. It's not easy to have to work and oversee a church for God. Just to work is a full-time job. All the same to oversee a church body of believers is quit a task in itself. With all the challenges of building and keeping the congregation focus in the high calling of God. But than its God that helps through His power to make all this possible.

When you chose to obey God and do what He wants you to do. Know that you're not able to stay A novice and preform the task at hand. You're going to either grow and mature or the task will break you. It's not a load you can carry without God's help.

Just recently as I was in prayer the Lord gave me a vision of a Huskey dog with its beautiful fur. His color was white with some grey and brown very healthy-looking dog. I found myself starring directly at him. As he sat strong winds blew swirling, but he didn't move. I could see it was cold and very windy. I wasn't understanding what God was trying to tell me by this vision. I thought maybe weather or hard conditions were coming. But wasn't certain what all this contain.

Around four months later and the spirit of the Lord brought it back to my remembrance. The interpretation came; God was showing me that whatever or however the challenges of rough conditions that were now here. Like those Huskey pure breed dogs that even if covered by snow they were able to survive the conditions. The odds being against them they could still manage to find their way home.

They were strong enough to overcome. God Was showing and telling me that He had done His preparations and like that Huskey, I was capable to overcome the challenges at hand. It had nothing to do with bad weather but that we are His workmanship with evidence of the heavens of God that we are His creation. To have faith and believe, because were made to overcome.

"Wrestles Against the Rulers of the Darkness"

Ephesians 6:11-12 Put on the whole armor of God, that you may be able to stand against the Wales of the devil; For we do not wrestle against flesh and blood but against the rulers of the darkness of this age, against spiritual hosts of wickedness in the heavenly places.

Our Lord Jesus Christ, our Heavenly Father, the King of Kings, through His Holy Spirit ask me to write on this topic (subject). I'm not sure what some think when reading this certain verse. **Wrestling against the rulers of darkness.** When we first receive our Lord and Savior, Born again Christian walk. The least thing we're thinking is fighting against spiritual wickedness. But God, knows what we'll need to overcome in battles ahead.

I had heard of witchcraft and on television voodoo was mentioned a lot. However, darkness in this earth has grown. By grown I mean, it's being used against people more than ever before. I'm aware many chose not to believe on such stuff. My reason of becoming familiar now more than ever. Is that our Lord Jesus Christ through His Holy Spirit has taught me and made me aware of how it's being used against the church of today. There's servants of God, preachers, pastors and Christians that have become sick, curse and broken by ruler of darkness. Because they don't fight spiritually against this type of spiritual darkness.

How can you fight against something you don't believe in. If Christians sin not or stay under the covering of the Lord righteousness. If they stay under the covering of the Lord Jesus Christ, and according to the **Living Word of God** under His statues. Then the power of darkness can't touch you or be effective against you. But that doesn't mean some people won't try to curse you. Or put witchcraft against you and even sent curses to curse your finances, health, marriages, work and list goes on. I have had good people, Christians come through the prayer line, not knowing why their always being sick. Some being told they must have done something wrong.

People are always ready to judge. But the things of spiritual are decern by the spirit. It's one thing to be born again and walk according to the word of the God. But to walk in the spirit and learn to decern in the spirit takes teaching. The Holy Spirit will teach you, but most of the time God's children have a hard time to just to be lead of the Spirit of God. Whatever they do, they make themselves believe that their being led by the Holy Spirit. It's one thing to do what you think is right. But to be led by the Holy Spirit, you need to learn to obey, follow, move according to what the Holy Spirit is asking you to do.

Some thirty years ago as I was praying in my home, I was asking God what was it that I could do for Him. I felt there was something that I could sense in my spirit I needed answers too. I heard the spirit of our Lord; if I sent you a drunk, will you minister unto him? If I sent you a drug addict, will you minister unto him? If I sent you a homosexual, will you minister unto him? And the Lord mention a few others, my reply was **yes** Lord I will. Then He ask me the same question again and again I answered **yes,** I will.

The Lord Jesus Christ replied I'm going to send them to you. I really wasn't sure what it all meant or would require of me. I was happy to be tested. Well, the Lord did send them, just as He said

He would. What we don't realize or think, is what all this intel's or requires a lot of patience, love for the lost and did I say a lot of patience. This people require a lot of your time. And not just regular hours there was this huge brother in the lord. He called himself a prophet but lacked the faithfulness part and the calling.

A few times my phone would ring around three in the morning. He was drunk and wanted me to go pray for him. I told him to wait until morning, when he wasn't so drunk. He got mad and very aggressive. At six am I went over to pray for him. And there he was still angry mad and pointing his finger at me. I did pray for him, but to overcome the illness of drinking, you need to want it and claim your deliverance by faith in the Lord's name. But what we're at times dealing with is lack of faith.

Also, the wanting to change and get rid of this wickedness for drinking. I've dealt with drug addicts, and all this is spirits keeping you blinded, we have delivered many from these addictions. The worst problem is people deny the problem.

On a church service I had a man come down the prayer line. I ask Him, what do you want prayer for? He had been in an accident. He said pray that I don't have so much pain. But don't pray that I get healed, because I'm still going through a settlement on the accident I had.

All these are normal situations we'll face, but by attending to this type of circumstances. The Lord was preparing me to look deeper into the cost of problems. It really takes a stronger discernment to open the eyes of your spirit. To start recognizing deeper problems that are hinderance in the world today. In our prayer groups as the anointing manifest some people in the group would start growling and making weird noises. Bad spirits don't like the anointing of God's spirit. So, they start acting up and get uncomfortable.

We would lay hands on them and start praying. It would take some time to deliver them. After much effort of prayer and time, they would get set free from whatever spirit they had. Something like that after years of delivering praying and helping deliver such people. Now it would take minutes because experience, but more the anointing of God given makes it faster. We through God's anointing have delivered some huge, strong ugly demons out of people.

After delivering many demons possess from the power of darkness. Many have become aware of our success in doing so. They or those that operate in the power of darkness have become familiar of our existence. We have broken curses that I would never had thought people could be so heartless. What's worst is that people go pay for the services of placing curses on people. Some of these curses can kill people and are sent for that exact purpose.

Lately we've had people send curses to us. We find out cause God reveals what's been sent. Some curses, we break through God easily, but others require more focus and stronger anointing focus. It's happened a couple of times, my wife and I were sitting in our living room, when suddenly, we heard a heavy weight sound land on our roof top.

We both turned at the same time to look at each other to say, what was that? It was a loud heavy weight creature had just landed on our roof.

I stood up and said to my wife, lets pray. Surely a warlock spirit in the form of a dragon flying creature is visible through the spirit of God. You might think I'm making this up; but those creatures, warlock, figures, dragon flying creatures and more, that you see in movies, where do you think those ideas come from. They didn't just come up with such a creature. Reason we know is that we had to fight against those things in the spiritual world, and that world is here on earth in high principality of darkness. It's above earth, but before heaven.

The only reason I'm on this subject is God wants His people to wake up and know there's a huge spiritual battle that exist. The way churches get together and pray as the word says, they are beating down strong holds. Well, the devil has his head quarters of rulers of darkness commanding people here on earth, working the people on earth. Because when his sent into hell with him he wants to take as many souls as he can.

By now he knows that his not about to defeat God or the heavens of God. His nature is to destroy and steal and kill. Now tell me, do you still think that all this stuff doesn't go on. The devil has people working on earth, witches, warlocks, and other people he has deceived to follow him. Why would they do this, because they like power and riches and control; but what they forget to understand the devil doesn't give anything for nothing. And yes, he believes in collecting what he claims belongs to him.

We have delivered people that used to work for the devil. But he doesn't give up so easy as people think. He'll make them sick and puts pressure on them. They refuse and he makes problems for trying to make them give up of this new walk with Jesus Christ.

However, my main point is for people to realize that preaching, teaching the word of God is great. Pastoring and having God's children under your leadership is great. But what about those in your membership that need a deeper help. That are suffering from spirits that have been attacking them all their lives. You might say, that's not your problem. But they are because when God called you and you said you would serve His will, whatever calling you might have. Takes obedience to serve.

You need to understand, these people that wouldn't hurt a fly The are good humble and wanting to overcome. But they don't know who to turn to. Most people, especially children that got rape are molested as a child. When that happen, whatever spirit was on the person doing the act of rape; that spirit entered the child raped. I know this because I have prayed for young men and women that were suffering from a spirit that entered them at the time of the act of molestation. Without them telling me anything.

At the moment that I laid hands on them to pray, the Lord through His spirit showed me the act. I would stop praying and address them not with a question, but how it happens. Some of these people are church members seeking help. But some churches are into entertainment. These people, they would buckle down with the fear and humiliation they had been fighting all this time. Finally, somebody understood and had some answers to why they felt how they felt.

We would pray and lead them to salvation, introducing them to realm of faith, salvation and a new walk with our Lord Jesus Christ. Just to inform you every time I say we, means my wife and I always work together. That gives me confirmation that I don't get into what I think but what were called to do, that's to operate in the fivefold ministry.

The fivefold gifts God gave unto the church to edify its members and believers. I do have my son and his wife working in the church ministry. Both my grandchildren, that are now in their twenties they also help in this type of ministry. When my wife and I would go visit families from the church and pray for them and their homes. Anything we were dealing with as we left the home.

My son was seven, eight, nine years of age. I remember since the first day we entered the ministry of the church, my son was always with us. After we would leave the certain homes, he would share what he saw spirits or things moving around that home. That made me aware that he had discernment at a very young age. Those spirits he had seen were exactly what was working in that home and family. We were very careful not allow anything to try and attack him, but yes all this is real, just because you have never seen or knew about this doesn't mean it's not real.

We didn't come into this looking for it. We came as servants of God. Ministers of the good news. As our grandchildren would go with us at a very young age my granddaughter, like my son was seeing spirits and things moving around homes. She would share with us, little by little we notice she had a gift of discernment. I would ask her questions to see if she was really discerning what was there.

As young as she was; but yes, she was decerning them exactly as they were. I'm sharing this with you, that you understand we're a real regular family. But we're moved to help the children of God. Plus, those that need help as well. I say this way, because there's a lot of people that don't want help nor believe, they say that they believe in God, but the word says none go before the Father but through the Son Jesus Christ. That means salvation, you need to be born again. Getting back to where I mentioned: church need help. Doctrines of God's word are good, baptism and a solid foundation. All these we're already supposed to be teaching. All these are the basics of walking with the Lord.

It's running a race that requires a little more. Let me explain, there's times I pray for people, God's children, sons, daughters of the faith. When I pray just over them with wishful thinking. By this I call it a simple prayer. Example: I pray healing over you. I pray you feel better, I pray this pain is completely healed. And sometimes in that form. This is praying for Christians. Yes, all done in the name of Jesus Christ, by faith and prayer. Now when gold miner goes digging, he uses a tool called a pic (it's an instrument) to break hard rock, ground and hard surface. A shovel bounces right off the surface. But the pic opens the hard surface.

When you pray and commit to focus than you can see the layers of rock build up over many years. Then there's also things blocking that prevent your prayer to be effective. But through faith, prayer and the anointing plus focus you can bypass the hinderance and remove whatever needs to remove spiritually.

To be more effective in the word of God to healing the individual. That's when you find the real cause of the problem. It can be a spirit causing pain, it can be a spirit causing infirmity, it can also be a curse or physical problem like blood flow, bad veins, bad heart, organs not working.

But when you know exactly what to call out of that person through the power of God's spirit His word they can be healed. We have had many people get healed, delivered and made whole. But again, all this connects with the gifts God gives to certain individuals. Gifts to edify the body of Christ until we all come into the unity of faith.

One God, One Lord, One Spirit, and One High Calling.

That dirt pic I mentioned earlier (for breaking hard ground) when you use this instrument, and the dirt is hard every time you slam that tool into the ground you feel a pull in your stomach. When you brace and make strength. Well in prayer when praying for someone with deeper prayer.

You use your faith and speak the word, but it requires more, the stronger making extra effort to help release individual from their need, pain or illness. You will feel a sharp pain in your stomach from your effort of prayer. Which means you give of God's virtue in you.

The Lord has sent His **Prophets, Apostles**, and **Preachers** led by His Spirit. But it's up to us to listen. We have witnessed an increase of the works of the Holy Spirit. An increase of the Holy Ghost and power. We have witnessed an increase of God's word being revealed unto us. The teaching of God's word with the manifestation of **Signs** and **Wonders.**

I pray this book will help and give you a desire to increase in the things God wants to do in your life.

God honor's faith and His word is faithful. There's a mighty work of God that awaits us in the days ahead.

One thing I have notice that man in churches use a lot of tricks, false doctrine and mostly their own ideas. But what's coming is that God's about to overturn tables in the body of the church.

Days of revealing His true servants in here now. The word says you'll know them by their fruits of the Spirit of God.